Science Alive

Materials

Terry Jennings

W
FRANKLIN WATTS
LONDON•SYDNEY

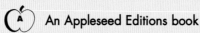 An Appleseed Editions book

First published in 2008 by Franklin Watts

Franklin Watts
338 Euston Road, London NW1 3BH

Franklin Watts Australia
Level 17/207 Kent St, Sydney, NSW 2000

© 2008 Appleseed Editions

Appleseed Editions Ltd
Well House, Friars Hill, Guestling, East Sussex TN35 4ET

Created by Q2A Media
Series Editor: Honor Head
Book Editor: Katie Dicker
Senior Art Designers: Ashita Murgai, Nishant Mudgal
Designer: Harleen Mehta
Picture Researcher: Poloumi Ghosh
Line Artists: Indernil Ganguly, Rishi Bhardhwaj
Illustrators: Kusum Kala, Sanyogita Lal

ISBN   978 0 7496 7565 3

Dewey classification: 620.1'1

All words in **bold** can be found in 'Words to remember' on pages 30-31.

Website information is correct at time of going to press. However, the publishers cannot
accept liability for any information or links found on third-party websites.

A CIP catalogue for this book is available from the British Library.

Picture credits
t=top b=bottom c=centre l=left r=right m=middle
Cover Images: Main Image: Kate Mitchell/zefa/Corbis; Small Image: Matka Wariatka/ Shutterstock
Michael Dwyer/Alamy: 4, Maxim Petrichuk/ Shutterstock: 7, Macduff Everton/ Corbis: 10, Shooterguy/ istockphoto: 11t,
Imageegaml/ istockphoto: 11b, Anthony Bolan/ Shutterstock: 12, ajt/ Shutterstock: 14m, Edward Hardam/
Shutterstock:14b, W. Cody/ Corbis: 15tr, TOMPKINSON GEOFF/ Photolibrary: 15bl, TAOLMOR/ Shutterstock: 18,
luxxtek/ istockphoto: 19, Charlie Drevstam/ Photolibrary: 20bl, whiteshadephotos/ istockphoto: 21, YinYang/
istockphoto: 24bl, Odin M. Eidskrem/ Shutterstock: 24bm, Timothy Large/ Shutterstock: 24br, George Hunter/
Photolibrary: 25tr, Geoffrey Kuchera/ Shutterstock: 25bl, TWPhoto/ Corbis: 28, Will & Deni McIntyre/ Corbis: 29

Printed in China

Franklin Watts is a division of Hachette Children's Books

Contents

Using materials

Every day we need food and drink, a roof above our head and clothes to wear. These are just a few examples of things that are made from materials.

Materials everywhere

Look around and have a think about all the different materials in the world. Wherever you go, you will see objects that are made from materials.

▲ *These people, buildings and vehicles are made from materials.*

Different states

The materials around us are solids, liquids or gases. For example, wood is a solid, oil is a liquid and the air that we breathe is a mixture of gases.

Ice

Steam

Water

▲ *Some materials change their **state** when they are heated or cooled. Liquid water becomes a solid (ice) when it is frozen and becomes a gas (steam) when it is heated.*

Material sources

Some materials come from natural sources, such as animals, plants or the ground. Sometimes, new materials are made from a combination of these sources. We call them man-made materials.

Material types

When we make something, we have to choose materials that are suitable for the job we are trying to do.

The right choice

Imagine a bed made from concrete – it would be very uncomfortable! Or imagine a window made from iron – it would be impossible to look through. There are much better materials available to make these objects.

▲ *This crash mat is firm, but soft enough for the gymnast to land on.*

Testing materials

Scientists test new materials to see if they are right for the job. Sometimes the materials are stretched or squashed thousands of times. These tests show how strong the materials are and what will happen to them when they are being used.

▲ *The frame of this bicycle is made of steel, which is strong but light. The tyres are made of rubber filled with air. They help the bicycle to ride smoothly.*

Try this...

Waterproof materials

Find out which materials are waterproof.

You will need
• four material samples, all the same size (plastic, paper, wool, cotton) • four clean, see-through plastic beakers • four elastic bands • an eye-dropper or small measuring spoon • water

1 Stretch each of the materials tight over the plastic beakers. Hold each material in place with an elastic band.

2 Use an eye-dropper or measuring spoon to place an equal amount of water (about 5 ml) on each of the materials. Watch carefully.

3 After ten minutes, carefully remove the material from the top of each pot. How much water is there in each of the pots?

What happened?

Some materials are made by weaving lots of threads together. The gaps between the threads allow water to seep through. The wool and cotton have the largest gaps and allow most water to pass through. The paper becomes soggy and may allow a little water to pass through. The plastic has no gaps and will not allow any water to pass through.

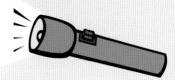

Glass

Glass was invented more than 4,000 years ago. We use glass in the windows of our buildings because it is see-through.

Making glass

Glass is made from sand and a chemical called lime. When glass is heated, it forms a sticky liquid that can be made into different shapes.

▲ *This man is shaping some hot glass into a jug. The glass will set hard again when it is cooled.*

Glass sheets

Melted glass can be poured into special tanks to make glass sheets. The glass spreads out like treacle and when it has cooled, it is solid enough to be taken away.

▶ *These windows have been made from glass sheets. The glass is very flat, smooth and thin.*

Safety glass

Glass is hard but it can break easily. Sometimes glass is strengthened to make it safer to use. Thin layers of glass and plastic are stuck together to make this 'safety glass'.

▲ *The safety glass in this car rear window has broken into tiny pieces. There are no sharp splinters that could cause harm.*

Wood

Wood comes from the trunks and branches of trees. Wood is a strong material and it can be easily cut and shaped.

World of wood

Some of our wood comes from trees with broad leaves, such as oak, beech and ash. The wood in these trees is very strong. Softer wood comes from forests of pine trees that have been planted because they grow very quickly.

▼ *When a tree is cut down you can see lots of rings in the wood. As a tree grows, a new ring forms each year.*

Using wood

Wood can be used to make houses, furniture and even paper. Wood is also used as a **fuel** because it burns very well when it is dry. When trees are cut into thick planks, the wood is dried slowly and carefully to stop it from bending. This is called **seasoning**. Sometimes the wood is dried in a special oven where warm air is blown between the planks.

▲ *Wood has been used to build boats for thousands of years. Wood is a strong material, but it is also light and can be shaped to float on water.*

Paper

Paper is one of the most common materials we use today. Paper is used in books, newspapers and magazines. But paper has other uses, too.

Useful paper

Paper is made from wood. We use it for writing and printing. Paper is also used for wrapping and packing. Other items made from paper include tissues, tickets, bank notes and posters.

◄ Take a look around and you will see lots of items made from paper. The book you are reading is made from paper, for example.

Making paper

Most paper is made from softwood trees, such as pine. Machines cut the wood into small pieces called chips. The wood chips are mixed with chemicals and made into a **pulp**, which is then cleaned with water.

▲ *Softwood trees are good for making paper. They grow quickly and are cheaper than hardwood trees, such as oak.*

From pulp to paper

At a paper factory, the wood pulp is spread out on to a wire screen. Heavy rollers squeeze out the water and press the pulp into a thin sheet. The paper is then dried by hot rollers and wound into an enormous roll.

◀ *A paper-making machine turns wood pulp into paper.*

15

Try this...

The strength of paper

Compare the strengths of different types of paper.

You will need
• sheets of different kinds of paper (such as tissue paper, newspaper, greaseproof paper) • a clean metal can • elastic bands • a clean yoghurt pot • small weights or marbles

1 Lay the tissue paper over the top of the tin can. Fix it in place with an elastic band.

2 Put the yoghurt pot on top of the tissue paper. Gently put weights or marbles, one at a time, into the yoghurt pot. How many weights do you add before the tissue paper breaks? Repeat with the other types of paper.

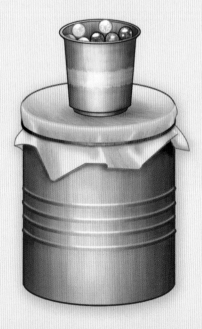

3 Now repeat the experiment, but this time wet each of the papers slightly first. Do you get the same results? Which is the strongest dry paper? Which is the strongest wet paper?

What happened?

The weakest paper is the one that breaks when the smallest number of weights is put in the yoghurt pot. The tissue paper is probably the weakest type of paper, when it is both wet and dry. One of the thick papers, such as greaseproof paper, is likely to be the strongest.

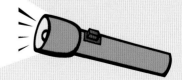

Plastic

Plastic is made from chemicals, most of which come from oil. Plastic is cheap and easy to make, and many different types are now available.

Plastics all around

Today, we often use plastics instead of materials such as wood, metal and glass. Some plastics are hard and stiff, while others are soft and bendy. Plastics are light, they do not **rust** or rot away, and many plastics are difficult to break.

▶ *This racing driver's helmet is made of strengthened plastic, while his gloves are made of a plastic that does not burn. Most of the car's body is also made of plastic.*

Using plastics

Buckets, bowls, bottles and toys are just a few of the things shaped from plastics. Some plastics can be drawn out into fine **fibres**. They can be mixed with other materials to make clothes. Other plastics can be made into flat sheets and used instead of glass.

▼ *Plastics can be coloured and moulded into many different shapes. This picnic set can be easily cleaned and will not break if it is dropped.*

Fibres and fabrics

Fabric is another word for cloth. We make fabrics by weaving or knitting together thin threads, called fibres.

Strength in numbers

One fibre is not very strong. But when fibres are spun together they can be made into a thread or rope, or they can be woven into fabrics.

▲ *This thread is made from three fibres spun together.*

◀ *Fabrics are all around us – from clothes and carpets to bedding and blankets.*

Natural fibres

Many fibres come from natural sources, such as animals or plants. Cotton comes from the seed pods of the cotton plant. Linen comes from the stem of the flax plant. Wool comes from the hair of sheep and other animals, while silk comes from fibres made by silkworms.

▶ *This sheep is being sheared for its wool. Wool is a useful material for clothing because it keeps us warm. Wool is also easy to cut and dye, and weave or knit.*

Artificial fibres

Artificial silk or rayon is made from wood pulp. Rayon is often mixed with wool or cotton to make clothes. Another man-made fibre is **nylon**. Nylon is made from chemicals that come from coal or oil.

21

Try this...

Testing fabrics

Test different fabrics to see which are the most hard-wearing.

You will need

• a thick newspaper • a large, rough stone • different types of fabric (such as cotton, nylon, denim) all the same size (strips about 15 cm wide and 30 cm long are easiest to handle)

1 Spread the newspaper on a table or desk to protect the surface. Lay the stone on the paper.

2 Take a piece of fabric. Hold one end in each hand and rub the fabric backwards and forwards across the stone. Count how many rubs it takes for a small hole to appear.

3 Now do the same thing with the other pieces of fabric. For your test to be fair, you must use equally hard rubs on each fabric. Which fabric is the most hard-wearing?

What happened?

Holes appear in the fabric when the rough edges of the stone break off little pieces of fibre. The hardest-wearing fabric takes the most rubs before a hole appears. This could be a synthetic fabric, such as nylon, or a heavy cotton fabric, such as denim.

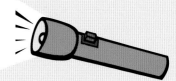

Metals

Metals, such as iron, copper and aluminium, are usually hard and shiny materials that can be bent and hammered into different shapes.

Useful metals

Steel is a strong metal made from iron. Many cars are made from steel. Aluminium is a strong, light metal which can be rolled into thin sheets without breaking. Copper and aluminium are good **conductors** of heat. They are often used to make pots and pans.

▲ Metals are all around us. This copper saucepan, steel can and roll of aluminium foil are all made from metals.

Metal ores

Most metals are found in rocks in the ground. Rocks that contain metals are called **ores**. They can be found deep underground, or near to the surface.

▲ *Special machines are used to dig into the ground to get the ores we need.*

Liquid metal

Some ores are heated in a large furnace (a big oven). This separates the metal from the rock. When the metal melts, it can be poured away to make different products.

◄ *This molten iron has been separated from its ore. When the iron cools it becomes a hard metal.*

Try this...

Heat conductors

Find out how heat passes through some materials better than others.

You will need
- a rubber hot-water bottle • water
- a piece of wood • a clock or watch
- a metal baking tray • a plastic plate
- a sheet of paper • a piece of cloth

1 Ask an adult to fill the hot-water bottle with hot (but not boiling) water. Carefully lay the hot-water bottle on the table. Quickly touch the outside of the bottle. Does it feel hot?

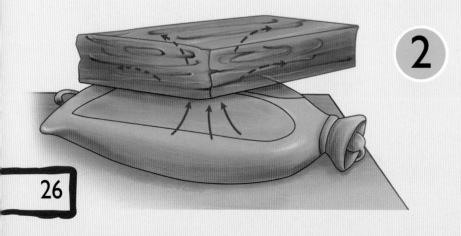

2 Lay the piece of wood on top of the bottle. Leave it there for four minutes. Does the wood feel hot, warm or cool now?

3 Now lay the metal baking tray on top of the hot-water bottle. Leave it there for four minutes. Is it hotter or colder than the wood was? Now test the other materials.

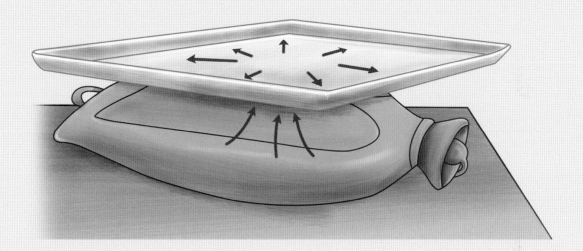

What happened?

The metal baking tray gets hot quickly because it is a good conductor of heat. The wood, plastic plate, paper and cloth allow heat through much more slowly. These materials are good **insulators** of heat.

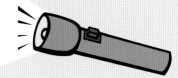

Recycling

Using materials again is called recycling. If we **recycle** materials instead of throwing them away, materials will last much longer.

Our daily rubbish

Every day, people throw away glass jars and bottles. We dump old cars, machinery and metal containers. If we keep throwing away materials like this, soon there will be none left.

▲ *Most of our rubbish is put in large holes in the ground like this. In the future we may run out of places to put our rubbish.*

Reusing materials

The best way to get rid of waste materials is to find another use for them. Waste paper and rags can be used to make paper and cardboard. Old jars and bottles can be used to make new glass. Metals can be melted down and moulded into different products.

◀ *At this recycling centre, glass, paper, metals and plastics are collected so the materials can be used again.*

Words to remember

Artificial
Something that
is man-made.
Some artificial
materials are
made from
chemicals.

Conductors
Materials through
which heat or
electricity can
pass easily.

Fibres
Long, thin,
hair-like strands.
Fibres are
woven together
to make a
fabric.

Fuel
Any material,
such as coal, oil,
gas or wood,
which will burn.

Insulators
Materials
through which
heat or
electricity do
not pass easily.

Nylon
A man-made
material made
from fibres that
are produced
from coal or oil.

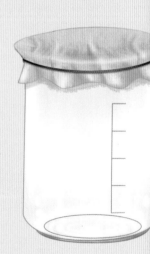

Ores
Rocks with a lot of metal in them.

Plastic
A material made from chemicals that come from oil.

Pulp
A soft, thick, wet mixture.

Recycle
To use again. Materials can be recycled instead of being thrown away.

Rust
A chemical reaction that causes metal to wear away.

Seasoning
The slow, careful drying of wood before it can be used to make things.

State
Materials can be found in one of three states – solid, liquid or gas.

Index

Webfinder

http://www.bbc.co.uk/schools/ks2bitesize/science/materials.shtml

http://www.bbc.co.uk/schools/scienceclips/ages/5_6/sorting_using_mate.shtml

http://www.bbc.co.uk/schools/digger/7_9entry/8.shtml

http://www.catie.org.uk/testing_time_index.html

http://www.crickweb.co.uk/assets/resources/flash.php?&file=materials2d

http://www.strangematterexhibit.com/